PAY YOURSELF FIRST

A FINANCIAL GUIDE
FOR DOCTORS ENTERING PRACTICE

DAVID A. BURD, CFP®
& JAMES S HEMPHILL, CFP®, CIMA

Published By:
TGS Financial Advisors
170 N. Radnor Chester Rd.
Radnor, PA 19087

www.tgsfinancial.com

TABLE OF CONTENTS

Introduction 1

Chapter 1: You've Made It 5

Chapter 2: Inflection Point 7

Chapter 3: A Tale of Two Doctors 11

Chapter 4: What is Wealth? 15

Chapter 5: The Trap of Status 19

Chapter 6: You Want a Piece of Me? 23

Chapter 7: Pay Yourself First 27

Chapter 8: Bending the Curve 33

Chapter 9: Investors Behaving Badly 39

Chapter 10: A Simple Plan 45

Chapter 11: The Seven Strategies 51

Chapter 12: The Advisor Advantage 55

Afterword 59

About the Authors 61

Disclosure

As physicians understand only too well, we live in a world of litigation and regulation. For this reason, and to protect you as a reader, we offer the following legal cautions:

David A. Burd, CFP and James S. Hemphill, CFP are Managing Directors of TGS Financial Advisors, an SEC registered investment advisor located in Radnor Pennsylvania. They have written this book as an introduction to the financial challenges faced by physicians beginning practice.

The intent of this book is to help you to understand the financial landscape, not to give you a detailed roadmap to your own individual destination. No reader should regard this book as the receipt of, or a substitute for, personalized advice from Mr. Burd, Mr. Hemphill, or from TGS Financial Advisors, or from any other investment professional.

Please remember that different types of investments involve varying degrees of risk. Therefore, it should not be assumed that the future performance of any specific investment, investment product, or investment strategy (including the investments and/or investment strategies referenced in this book), or any of the book's non-investment related content, will be profitable, prove successful, or be applicable to any individual's specific situation.

Should a reader have any questions about how to apply the principles in this book to his or her individual situation, the reader is encouraged to consult with the professional advisors of his or her choosing.

Introduction

"If I was doing this job to make money, I would not be doing this job."

Neonatologist
Pacific Northwest

"The only way not to think about money is to have a great deal of it."

Edith Wharton

Some years back I was on the Board of a local non-profit. I was brought in to help solve the school's perpetual financial crisis. Over several years, we put financial controls in place, recruited more committed and generous Board members, secured new sources of funding, and began a systematic fund-raising program.

During those rebuilding years, most of our conversation on the Board was about money, not mission. We had no ability to improve programs because all of our energy was consumed with finding enough dollars to keep the doors open.

One of my take-aways from this experience was that being short of money can dominate your thought, in a way that interferes with matters of much greater meaning.

I know no physicians who chose their careers for strictly monetary reasons. Many knew they wanted to be doctors before their understanding of finances went beyond how many comic books they could buy with a week's allowance.

The greatest rewards of being a physician, according to the physicians we know, are those arising from the practice of medicine itself – the chance to work with capable peers, to save lives and improve their quality, to create profound value in the world.

The worst aspect of contemporary medicine, according to pretty much every physician we know, is the endless paperwork and time concerned with who gets paid, how much and when, by which third-party, for doing what to whom.

I'm entirely persuaded by the idea that money must be secondary to a physician's mission. Yet as a financial advisor with doctors as clients and as friends, I'm also very much aware of two things:

> Doctors as a group significantly under-perform most other professions at accumulating wealth, in relation to their incomes.

> Many doctors worry, chronically and seriously, about their own personal money situations.

This book is intended to provide some guidance about how to deal with money issues, systematically and sensibly, from the very beginning of your career, so that money can occupy its proper place in your life – as background noise that does not distract from the real sources of joy, satisfaction and contribution – your career, family, friends and patients.

Jim Hemphill
Radnor, PA
Summer 2013

After years of schooling and punishing workdays of twelve or more hours during residency and fellowship, you are ready to start your career as a medical specialist. You will finally begin to reap the financial rewards you deserve for your decades of hard work.

Chapter 1: You've Made It

As a new specialist physician, you have deferred gratification like few other professionals on earth. You have excelled in every academic environment, graduating at the top of your class from high school, college and medical school, won a prized fellowship, and then worked insane hours as a resident and fellow for ridiculously low wages.

By the time you finish a fellowship in a medical sub-specialty, you will have spent up to 16 years in schooling after high school, and invested more than 30,000 hours in classwork, residency and fellowship. (A thoracic surgeon may spend almost 50,000 hours in education and training, not including non-class study hours.)

If you were paid $50,000 a year as a fellow, working 80 hours per week, you earned as little as $12.50 per hour, less than the waiter at the local tavern on a busy Friday night. Plus, a typical fellow has accumulated more than $170,000 in school loans.

You are now in a position, for the first time, where your contributions are going to be fairly rewarded. In the Mid-Atlantic states, where our financial advisory practice is located, a new cardiac surgeon might see her income increase from $50,000 as a fellow to $300,000 when she is hired by a cardiovascular surgery practice.

You need to make sure that those increased economic rewards will provide the maximum benefit, for you and your family, over your entire lifetime.

Reading this book should take you less than one hour. We hope it may benefit you for decades to come.

Within one year of beginning practice as a physician, you will make the key choices that will either place you on a path toward financial independence, or establish a high-consumption lifestyle you may be unable to sustain without working, even as you approach normal retirement age.

Chapter 2: Inflection Point

"This is not the end, or even the beginning of the end. But it might just be the end of the beginning."

Winston Churchill

What Churchill described in June of 1942 was the inflection point in World War II. Within weeks, the British defeated Rommel's Afrika Korps at El Alamein, the Russians destroyed the German Army Group Center at Stalingrad, and the U. S. Navy broke the back of Japan's carrier air fleet at the Battle of Midway. That inflection point was not the end of struggle and sacrifice. But it was a crucial, and permanent, change of direction.

Now you face your personal inflection point. The transition from fellowship to practice in a medical specialty is likely to be the single most financially significant event in your life. The decisions you make within one year of starting practice will largely determine the arc of your financial future.

Of course, the choices you are about to make are only the latest in a lifelong series, each of which has altered the trajectory of your life:

> ➤ The first time you thought, "I want to be a doctor when I grow up."

> ➤ The point when you decided to take more challenging high school courses in order to get into a better college.

> ➤ When you declared your college major, choosing Biology or another hard science, and submitting to

the rigors and competition of the pre-med curriculum.

> Your choice to defer your first big payday (again) by pursuing and accepting a challenging fellowship.

Each of these decisions is best understood not as an *event*, but as the beginning of a *process*. Each choice was followed by commitment, action, event and consequence.

Now all of those choices have borne fruit. Your income has increased several hundred percent, and your new challenge is deciding how to allocate that increased income. The default choice, for physicians as for American society as a whole, leans heavily toward immediate consumption. The alternative choice balances consumption today against financial independence tomorrow.

Choosing financial independence creates challenges both financial and psychological, which we will explore more fully in the coming pages. Don't be discouraged. If you are willing to put in place the necessary habits and financial structures, then in the following chapters we will outline how you can take your first steps along a path toward achieving walk-away wealth by the time you are sixty years old.

Regardless of the financial choices you make in the coming weeks and months, you will do challenging and valuable work, with peers who are among the most capable individuals on the planet. You will bring healing and comfort to your fellow humans for decades to come, saving lives and improving health.

All of this is good. *Don't ignore the power of choice at the inflection point.*

All names have been changed, and the stories of different individuals have been combined to form composites, in order to carefully protect client confidentiality. The two narratives in this chapter are altered as to name, location and specialty, but the numbers given here are not hypotheticals or projections. They are the real results of real doctors.

Chapter 3: A Tale of Two Doctors

Marie and Edward were both anesthesiologists. They met at a medical conference and married in their thirties. They bought a charming home, built in the 1920s but recently remodeled, in an upscale suburb of Philadelphia, within easy commuting distance of the two hospitals where they worked.

Marie was a partner in an independent practice, while Ed was an employee of a large urban hospital. As anesthesiologists, both earned high incomes, though not as high as those of some surgical sub-specialties. From early in their careers, each contributed the maximum allowed to their retirement plans at work. Marie's partnership made the maximum employer contribution to her plan as well, and she saved at least another 10% of her income to after-tax accounts. Both invested primarily in common stocks.

Their two children went to public schools in their highly-rated school district. They bought a cottage on a lake in the mountains. They vacationed mostly at their cottage, though they took an occasional trip to Europe or Disney World.

Marie worked with a financial advisor from the beginning of her career. Ed managed his funds himself until they began to consider early retirement, then began to work with the same advisor.

At age 58, with the younger child in college, Ed went to half-time work. They bought a three-story row house in the historic Society Hill section of Philadelphia, which they gutted and re-built, with Ed supervising construction. They installed an elevator, a wine cellar, and enough bookshelves for Marie's thousands of books.

At Marie's age 58, Ed's age 61, with both kids done college, they walked away, retiring from medical practice, selling their house in the suburbs and moving into the city, near the music and culture they loved. Their net worth was over $8 million. They looked forward to decades of active retirement, without a hint of financial worry.

John was an orthopedist, and his wife Anne an attorney with her own practice. Based on John's high income, they bought a historically-significant mansion on Philadelphia's Main Line, where they raised three children, all of whom went to exclusive and expensive private schools.

Starting in the 1980s, John saved the maximum personal amount to his 401k, but he and his partners could never agree about whether they wished to cover employees in their retirement plan, and his practice did not make any employer contributions.

They regarded Anne's income as their "vacation money," and did not save much of it. Anne did not set up any employer-based retirement plan, though she did make occasional contributions to an Individual Retirement Account. John managed their investments, and lost significant funds when the tech bubble collapsed in the early 2000s.

In his late 50s, John experienced health problems, and had to retire from his orthopedic practice. He transitioned into medical administration, at a reduced salary. At the same time, Anne's legal practice began to wind down.

When both were age 62, they were referred to our advisory practice by a friend, another physician client. When we met them, their total investment net worth (excluding real estate but including all retirement assets) was less than $400,000.

We did a full financial proposal for them, targeting retirement at age 70 with an income level that would replace John's after-tax salary, an amount in the low six figures. Since all of their kids were grown and out of the house, we recommended they sell their big house and down-size to a condo. The net proceeds from the change of residence would have been over $500,000, to be added to their investment portfolio. We projected the annual savings on upkeep would be in excess of $40,000. Over the eight years until age 70, we hoped to help them build their portfolio to more than $1.5 million.

They never sold the big house, because they wanted plenty of bedrooms for when their grandchildren came to visit. John continued to make the maximum annual contribution to his 401k each year, but Anne began to draw down her IRA to pay for several weddings. Seven years later, their investment net worth had grown to just over $600,000.

John has now retired, and Anne has closed down her legal practice. Their investments will supplement their Social Security to provide retirement cash flow, with total annual income under $100,000. They hope their investment assets will last for at least ten years, at which time they will finally sell their house and downsize.

Their situation is a far cry from poverty. They have more assets, and will spend more income in retirement, than the majority of Americans. But this is surely not what they expected their retirement to look like, back in the 1990s at the peak of John's career, when their annual income was over half a million dollars.

The pattern of your life will be your own, but you are likely to find echoes of the lifestyle choices made by these two physician families, and of their financial consequences, in your own experience. One factor in particular is worth noting – *it is not your gross level of income that will buy you financial security; it is the decisions you make on how to allocate that income stream – the relative percentages directed toward consumption and toward savings.*

As a hard-working, high-earning specialist physician, you are going to be rich no matter what – by somebody's definition. You need to be sure that the definition of wealth you choose is the one that gets you the results you want, both here at the beginning of your career, and decades from now at the end.

Chapter 4: What is Wealth?

"Two roads diverged in a wood and I –
I took the one less-traveled by,
And that has made all the difference.

> Robert Frost
> The Road Not Taken

Your challenges are born of your own earned success and achievement. Your choices require deciding how to allocate a relative abundance of income and opportunity. The path you follow will depend on the definition of wealth that you choose. So let's ask two related, difficult questions:

> ➤ *What is wealth?*

> ➤ *Who is rich?*

When many Americans think of wealth, they picture Donald Trump, with his television show, bad hair, serial wives and multiple residences. In Trump's world, wealth is measured by the visibility of the material objects you display, by your own notoriety, and by the control you can exercise over other people.

In reality, there have been times when Trump has had negative net worth – he has actually *owed* more on his various projects and properties than he *owned*. But he never moved out of the mansion with the gold-plated bathroom fixtures, or stopped getting his $200 bad haircuts.

If you want to be financially-independent, you're going to need a better concept of wealth. Here's our working definition: *You are rich when you can maintain the lifestyle you choose, for as long as you live, without ever being required to work.*

There are two key components of this definition:

> ➤ You *define* your target lifestyle. The cost of that *chosen* lifestyle determines the capital needed to sustain it indefinitely.

> ➤ You will be targeting walk-away wealth, but you will not be required to actually walk away once you attain it.

Let's examine the relationship between lifestyle and capital:

> ➤ A cardiac surgeon who chooses a lifestyle featuring a mansion in a posh suburb, a beachfront home at the shore, a new Mercedes every three years for each spouse, and annual European villa vacations with the extended family, might need an investment portfolio worth $20 million to be "rich" by our functional definition.

> ➤ A public schoolteacher whose defined lifestyle includes a modest house in a good school district, who drives the same car for 200,000 miles and vacations in a tent at a National Park, who can expect a taxpayer-funded public pension and lifetime medical benefits, might be functionally rich with less than $500,000 of investment assets.

How can the person with much less income and lower net worth be functionally richer? *Because she can walk away and keep it all going.*

Your chosen lifestyle will probably fall between these extremes. Still, you should be highly intentional about that lifestyle, because *it is your choice of lifestyle that will determine the target wealth needed to sustain it indefinitely.*

Next, let's examine the idea of walk-away wealth. Keep in mind that attaining true financial independence does not require you to stop working. (Consider Warren Buffett, worth $55 billion and still going to work at Berkshire Hathaway every day at age 82.)

Here's a narrative we often hear from younger doctors: "I don't need to be financially independent at age 60, because I plan to keep working into my 70s."

Maybe yes, and maybe no.

Historically, physicians were among the least likely professionals to seek early retirement. Who would want to leave the high-prestige, intellectually challenging, psychologically-rewarding job of healer? As recently as the late 1980s, the average physician did not retire until after age 70. Yet a 2012 survey by the Physicians Foundation found that over 60% of doctors would retire today if they had the financial means, an increase of one-third in only four years.

Based on more than a quarter-century of working with doctors, we suspect the chance you will wish to retire early is greater than you think now, at the beginning of your career. The career choices of physicians have changed as medicine has become more bureaucratized, as paperwork increases even as clinical autonomy decreases, as reimbursements decline while treatment expectations rise, and as the amount of uncompensated medical care continues to increase.

We hope your medical practice will be so rewarding that you will choose to practice into your 70s, even if you have the wealth to walk away at 60. We certainly understand that our nation faces a looming shortage of physicians. But just in case medical practice becomes even more stressful, we like the idea you might be able to regard your work as a free choice, and not as a perpetual, involuntary economic necessity.

Doctors have a unique disadvantage in building wealth, because they are expected to display wealth and status. With no other profession are such high incomes associated with such low rates of financial independence. Here at the inflection point, you have the best opportunity of your life to increase your comfort and status, while still putting away much greater savings.

Chapter 5: The Trap of Status

"It is neither wealth nor splendor; but tranquility and occupation which give you happiness."

Thomas Jefferson

Nobody expects a plumber to drive a BMW and live in a big house. That doesn't mean there are no successful plumbers. Far from it. And surely there are many wealthy plumbers happily driving Bimmers and living large. But nobody *expects* it of them.

On the other hand, everyone has expectations of doctors – how they look, act, and dress, what they drive, where they live. Those peer expectations are powerful.

Human beings are primates, not rodents; we are chimpanzees more than squirrels. We are social, competitive, and status-oriented. We are hard-wired to keep up with the Joneses, much more than we are to save our acorns for the winter.

In evaluating our status, we compare ourselves to a peer group. Psychologists call this process *social comparison*. Initially, greater income is associated with greater happiness, though the law of diminishing returns surely applies. (Raising your income from $25,000 to $50,000 has way more psychic benefit than the identical dollar increase from $300,000 to $325,000.)

Unfortunately, that gain in happiness is often temporary. As people adapt to a new, higher level of status, they begin to compare themselves to a similarly successful peer group, and the psychic benefit of their elevated status erodes.

Spending on possessions has the most transient effect on

happiness, while spending on relationships and experiences has more durable emotional benefits. Unlike status based on *earning* or *spending*, research suggests that attaining $1 million of *net worth* is associated with a permanent increase in confidence and self-esteem.

The default choice for most young doctors is to spend now and save later. Spending today responds to powerful signals in our culture, and fulfills compelling status expectations. So why *not* spend your available cash flow now, getting your household established and making up for lost time, and get around to saving later?

Just as the 'spend now' strategy fulfills status expectations, the 'save later' aspect will violate them, since it will eventually require a painful reduction in displayed wealth, comfort and status. Ignore the purely practical sacrifices. (At the peak of your career, do you really think you will fancy trading in your Lexus for a Toyota Camry?) The psychic cost of reducing spending sharply, in order to catch up on retirement savings, would be profound.

Unfortunately, the relationship of wealth to happiness is asymmetric. Moving up is often only temporarily rewarding. But losing ground – suffering even a limited reduction in socio-economic status – is durably painful.

Given the limited half-life of the joys of an enhanced lifestyle, we suggest retaining a healthy baseline skepticism about status. After all, you are not required to meet anyone else's expectation of how you live. Not your mother's, your colleagues', society's, nor those of your Mercedes Benz salesman, real estate broker or financial advisor.

Remember, the highest status activity you engage in, and the highest value you contribute to the world, will always be simply your work as a physician.

As a specialist physician, your income will place you in the top 5% of American workers, yet here at the beginning of your career your assets are probably smaller than those owned by the average public school teacher. Asset poor and cash flow rich; in your first years of practice, everyone will want a piece of that cash flow.

Chapter 6: You Want a Piece of Me?

"Everyone wants to get a piece of me."

Tiger Woods

As a new medical specialist, you have a large amount of uncommitted cash flow. With lots of disposable income and a pristine credit history, banks will be eager to loan you money. Real estate agents will compete to show you big, beautiful houses. Car dealers will offer you top-tier lease terms on new Lexus or Mercedes automobiles.

We are a consumer-driven society. A clean, bright, well-lighted house in beautiful surroundings can be a lasting joy. A well-made luxury automobile appeals on many levels. Dinner at a fine restaurant with someone you love is one of life's great pleasures. With all of these positive goods, it is difficult to draw a bright line that says, 'This is enough.'

Yet just as income and status are subject to the law of diminishing returns, so are consumer goods. A Toyota is a nicer automobile than a Scion, and a Lexus nicer still. But the extra functionality you buy for the next $10,000 at the margin becomes ever smaller as the absolute price increases.

You should be especially cautious about debt. With interest rates near historic lows, right now it is particularly tempting to take on a large debt load. You may be able to service the 3.5% interest cost of a jumbo mortgage without breaking a sweat, but it will still take a generation to pay off the principal. Not only that, the larger house you buy with the bigger, cheaper mortgage will also come with higher operating expenses. Unlike the monthly fixed-rate mortgage payments, those operating costs will increase with inflation.

Among the goods that new doctors buy are financial services. Let's consider a specific not-so-hypothetical. Assume that in your first three months of work you have saved $20,000 and change. What should you do with it?

> ➤ If you buy a $500,000 face whole-life insurance policy with a first-year premium of $20,000, the insurance agent will earn a commission of $8,000.

> ➤ On the other hand, you could buy a $2 million twenty-year level-premium term life insurance contract for $1,100 per year, and invest almost $20,000 with an investment advisor. At a 1.5% annual advisory fee, the investment guy will earn $300 managing your portfolio over the first year. (Actually, he will lose money. That $300 will not cover the costs of opening accounts and mailing statements.)

Who has the greater incentive to chase after your business? Obviously, the insurance guy soliciting purchase of the whole-life insurance policy. Yet the fact that the insurance salesman has the greater incentive to pursue your business does *not* mean every element of his financial solution is optimal for you and your family.

Don't get us wrong. Protecting your earnings with disability insurance, your family with life insurance, your assets with liability insurance, and your career with malpractice insurance, are all foundations of your lifetime financial security. When we begin work with a new physician client, one of the first things we do is make a referral to the right insurance agent. We believe most doctors should put insurance protections in place *before* they begin building an investment portfolio. But you should own the right kind of insurance for your circumstances and career stage.

Plenty of other people are going to get well-paid based on the decisions you make. Amid the excitement of all the new opportunities, and the distraction of competing sales presentations, try to keep one principle in mind: *Pay yourself first*.

Whatever your cash flow, it will be easy to find opportunities to spend it. That is why you need to make savings your first priority, not the last. Of all of the components of a successful wealth-building program, none is more important than time.

Chapter 7: Pay Yourself First

"Work expands to fill the time allotted to its completion."

Parkinson's Law

Spending, like work, expands easily to consume all of the space available for it. Many doctors choose to acquire the house, the cars, the vacation home, and the rest of the lifestyle elements first, assuming they can take care of the savings later. Unfortunately, this sequence is problematic, for two reasons. As we've discussed, the first is the psychology of status; it is easy to move up, desperately unpleasant to move down.

The second is the magic – and tyranny – of compound interest. Consider two saving/spending sequences:

- ➤ Save 20% of your income starting at age 35, and continue through age 45, then stop. (Ten years of savings.)

- ➤ Spend your income when you begin practice at age 35, then start saving aggressively at age 45, putting away 20% of income, and continue through retirement at age 65. (Twenty years of savings.)

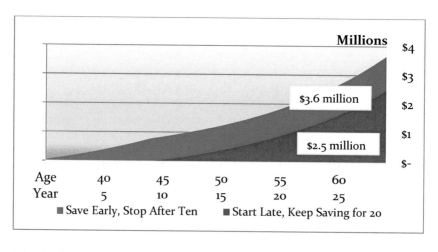

	Millions	
		$4
		$3
	$3.6 million	$2
		$1
	$2.5 million	$-

Age	40	45	50	55	60
Year	5	10	15	20	25

■ Save Early, Stop After Ten   ■ Start Late, Keep Saving for 20

Here's the same data set in table form[1]:

	Save Early, Stop After Ten	Start Late, Keep Saving for 20
Total Savings	$500,000	$1,000,000
Total Earnings	$3,146,147	$1,471,146
Ending Value	$3,646,147	$2,471,146
Savings % of Total	13.7%	40.5%

As you can see, the late saver does not ever catch up to the early saver, despite saving for twice as long and putting aside twice as many dollars out of income. *Almost 90% of the early saver's total wealth comes from earnings – from the compounding effect of money-making-money – while less than 60% of the late saver's wealth comes from compounding.*[2]

---

[1] In both the graph and the table, we are assuming gross income of $250,000, savings of $50,000 per year, and investment returns of 8% per year.

[2] Of course, there is no requirement to stop saving after ten years, and we don't recommend that anyone do so. In our example, if the early saver kept saving to age 65, she would accumulate over $6 million of investment net worth.

This is a hidden cost of medical training that most non-physicians simply cannot understand. Not only have you studied longer than any other professional, incurred hundreds of thousands of dollars in education loans, and deferred a serious payday until your mid-30s, you have also lost precious years of potential compounding on your savings.

We are *not* suggesting that you save for only ten years, and we are certainly not promising 8% annual returns. In fact, we expect long-term investment returns will be lower than normal over the next decade. But that means it is *more* important, not less, that you save significant amounts as soon as you can. *If you wait to start saving until you have acquired all of the things you want, you will lose precious compounding time you cannot make up later.*

In the last chapter, we discussed the difficulty of drawing a bright line at the ideal 'enough stuff' level. That is why you need to draw the line from the other direction. Start off by determining the savings rate you will need to reach your financial independence goal, and then put structures in place to make those savings happen, as reliably and automatically as possible. (More on this later.) Then you can decide how to allocate your remaining after-tax cash flow with a clear conscience and no misgivings.

Nobody expects you to drive a 1995 Honda Civic and live in a rental apartment. You can expect to live in a comfortable home, drive a new, safe car, and enjoy meals out and relaxing vacations. Will that car be a Toyota Camry, an Acura MDX or a 7-Series BMW? Will your home be a 3,000 square foot used house in a great school district, or a 6,000 square foot new-construction McMansion? Will vacation be a week at Disney World, or ten days skiing in Gstaad, Switzerland?

As financial advisors, we hate feeling as though we are in the position of saying, "Thou shalt not." Please understand that we are not making a moral judgment about which path you choose. Frankly, we believe you should buy what you darn well please. After all, you are the one who just finished long years of 11 hour workdays that would have brought us to our knees in a week. And the 7-

series BMW is one terrific automobile. You could drive us to California sitting in that back seat and we wouldn't mind.

But understand that, in weighing these choices, you are not negotiating with us. You are negotiating with yourself – your future self, in ten, twenty, even thirty years from now. The choices you make will determine the balance between the lifestyle that you enjoy today, and the lifestyle and the stress levels that you'll experience in your 50s, 60s, even in your 70s and beyond.

Which will you choose?

> ➢ I will have the most beautiful home, and the hottest car, of anyone I knew in college.

> ➢ I will have walk-away wealth before any of my medical school peers.

In twenty-five years, you can be the first of your peers with walk-away wealth. Or you can be age 60, living in a beautiful house, driving a luxury car, and worried that if you stop working you will run out of money within five years.

Politicians promise to "bend the curve," reducing future medical costs through various "reforms." Often this translates down the road into cuts in reimbursement rates for Medicare and Medicaid. There is another curve you need to bend *upwards* – the curve of compound wealth, carrying you toward financial independence. To do this, you must maximize the after-tax return on every savings dollar.

Chapter 8: Bending the Curve

"A penny saved is a penny earned."

Ben Franklin

Back in our grandparents' time, some number of virtuous people watched every nickel and dime they spent, saved a few precious dollars each week, and then stuffed those savings in the mattress, hid them in a cookie jar or deposited them at the local savings and loan.

This is the "pay yourself last" model of savings. With enough self-discipline, frugality, and foresight, you can follow this strategy and use it to build walk-away wealth.

Good luck with that. "Pay yourself last" is no longer a realistic strategy for savings. We live in a richer, safer world than our grandparents did, but also a more complex and confusing one, where the demands on our time, attention and financial resources are much greater. Few of us have that simpler world's emotional commitment to thrift. *If you plan to save whatever you have left at the end of the month, you are liable to end up out-of-money days before you are out-of-month.*

Instead, you should pay yourself *first*. To be most effective, savings should be:

➢ Automatic.

➢ Tax-efficient.

➢ Directed toward the highest available risk-adjusted, after-tax economic return.

Let's get very specific about how you can best use "pay yourself first" principles to build your wealth.

Your first priority should *always* be maximizing pre-tax savings to your employer retirement plan (401k, 403b, SEP, etc.). Those contributions will be withdrawn automatically from your paycheck, and your employer will often match a portion of your savings. This is "free money" in your account.

Let's examine why this type of savings is so effective, by looking at the after-tax consequence of directing $10,000 of income toward pre-tax vs. after-tax savings:[3]

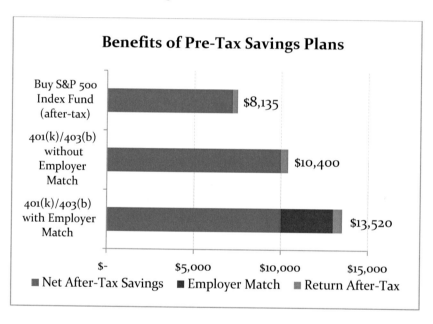

As you can see, over the course of a year, the pre-tax savings plan

---

[3] We are assuming gross income of $200,000, which suggests a 28% marginal tax bracket for a married couple. We are illustrating a 401k with a 50% employer match on the first $6,000 of savings, and assuming investment returns are on the low side at 4% per year. If income, tax rates and/or investment returns are higher, the pre-tax option becomes even more attractive.

with an employer match is very hard to beat.

For most of our physician clients, employer-based retirement savings plans have been the foundation of their financial independence, representing at their retirement the majority of their investment net worth. Those savings might be in the form of a 403(b) for doctors working for a non-profit hospital system, or of a 401(k) for those working for a for-profit hospital or medical practice. In some cases, those savings plans may be supplemented by a profit-sharing plan for the self-employed, or even (for a lucky few), by an actual pension benefit.

What if you buy into the central thesis of this book, and decide to really push savings? You have already maxed-out on all pre-tax employer savings opportunities, and you want to save additional dollars after-tax. Where should they go?

First, understand that a dollar of principal paid down against a debt has every bit as much effect upon your net worth as a dollar saved to a bank account. *Debt paydown is a form of savings, and sometimes the most effective form.*

With both direct savings and debt paydown on an equal footing, you should direct your after-tax savings dollars toward *the highest risk-adjusted after-tax return.*[4] Consider one set of possible choices:

➢ Pay down a non-deductible medical school loan at 6.9%.

➢ Pay down your home mortgage, which costs you a tax-deductible 4.5%. (An after-tax cost of 3.2 %.)

---

[4] The tax code gets ever more complex. Depending on income, the tax rate on dividends and capital gains could be as low as 0% and as high as 23.8%. Your mortgage interest might be fully-deductible, or entirely non-deductible. The devil is in the details, and the nature of the tax devil changes frequently and capriciously. Hence the importance of the *principle* of after-tax return, rather than the specific sequence offered here.

> Buy a bank CD at 1.5%, with no market risk.

> Buy a stock index fund in a taxable account, with a projected return of 4% per year, with market risk.[5] (An implied after-tax return of 3.3%, assuming 18.8% tax rates on dividends and capital gains.)

Here is a visual of this opportunity set:

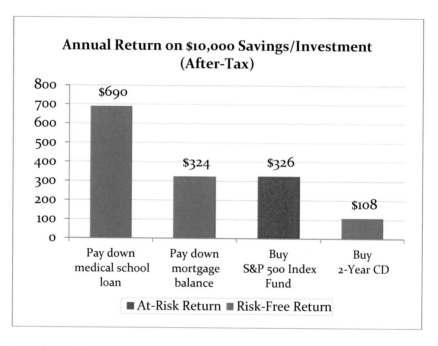

Based on the principle of highest after-tax, risk-adjusted return, the optimal sequence looks like this:

> The highest return available to you is a risk-free 6.9%, by paying down medical school loans.

> Once those loans are paid off, the stock fund and the mortgage "pay" a similar after-tax return of just over

---

[5] We'll discuss how to think about market returns in Chapter 10.

3.2%, but the return on mortgage paydown is risk-free, so paying down mortgage principal is the better choice.

So 401k first, school loans second, mortgage third and stock fund fourth. The bank certificate, yielding just over 1% after-tax, has no place in your portfolio.

Keep in mind that this sequence is based upon a specific fact-pattern, at a specific point in time, under a specific tax regime. Given different interest rates, financial markets conditions, or tax rates, an entirely different sequence of savings might make more sense. But the principle would be unchanged – *always direct dollars to the highest risk-adjusted after-tax opportunity*.

You have now determined how much savings, as a percentage of income, you intend to put away, and you have also determined the optimal sequence of savings. What is the best way, practically, to set up your savings plan?

Just as with pre-tax retirement plan savings, which come out of your paychecks before you even see them, you should make your other savings happen as automatically as possible.

Most employers can set up auto-payments to multiple bank accounts. Set up one "master savings" account, and have your employer direct a fixed percentage of your compensation to it. From this account, make automatic transfers to pay down loans, build cash in a reserve account, fund 529 college savings accounts, or buy investments.

Your objective is to shift enough income from your paycheck to fund all of your savings priorities, before any money ever gets to any account from which you spend.

Once you have all of the elements of your automatic savings plan in place, you can then decide how to spend your remaining after-tax cash flow with a clear conscience and no misgivings.

Understand that Wall Street's promise of superior investment performance rarely comes true for individual investors. Instead of counting on high investment returns to build wealth, aim for high savings rates.

Chapter 9: Investors Behaving Badly

"First, do no harm."

Hippocratic Oath

The Father of Medicine's advice to physicians, back in the 5th century B. C., is also sound counsel for investors today. Better to do nothing than to do something harmful – and the data clearly show that most active investing strategies do harm; they subtract from portfolio returns rather than adding to them.

Here is the data on mutual fund investor performance from research firm DALBAR, for the twenty-year period ending December 31, 2012:[6]

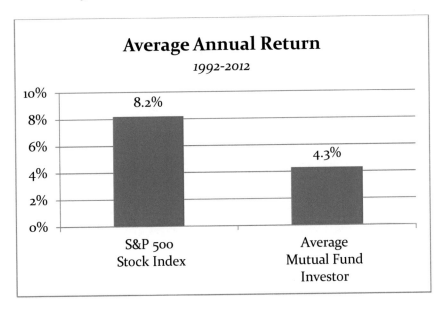

---

[6] *DALBAR Quantitative Analysis of Investor Behavior 2013.*

Understand what these data mean – it is not that the typical mutual *fund* underperformed the market by 48%. It is that the typical *investor* in mutual funds underperformed – by choosing the wrong funds, by being in or out of the market at the wrong times, by chasing performance in up markets and panicking during down markets – in short, by trying to do *better* than the markets, investors did much *worse*.

But wait a bit. You are not some Average Joe or Jane off the street. You are a physician, the brightest of the bright. Obviously, you will do better than average, right?

Wrong, almost certainly. Most individuals make decisions about their investments that are remarkably sub-optimal. Research in the emerging discipline of behavioral economics suggests that these poor outcomes are not the result of *cognitive* deficits, nor are they *informational* disadvantages. They are powerful, persistent and intrinsic *behavioral* biases.[7]

In other words, being whip-smart won't save you from being greedy or fearful, nor will it cure you of confirmation bias, framing effects or attribution errors.

Consider one central insight of behavioral economics: *Most individuals are over-confident about almost everything, almost all the time.* In general, this over-confidence is a survival trait. Who would have asked their future spouse out on a date, cultivated a potato, eaten an oyster, crossed the oceans to the New World, written a first novel, or signed up to take the MCATs, without healthy self-confidence?

Unfortunately, over-confidence can be deadly for investors, since long-term investment success is based largely on a disciplined

---

[7] In fact, some data on identical twins raised in separate households appears to demonstrate that investment success is largely based on innate psychological traits, not on experience or training. (In other words, Warren Buffett was born, not made.)

understanding of what we can and cannot predict.

Yet if there is one essential characteristic of most physicians, it is self-confidence. This is particularly true of surgical specialists. If you are poised above someone's left ventricle, scalpel in hand, you had better not be paralyzed by self-doubt.

That sort of robust confidence simply isn't an asset for an investor. Successful investing requires both a different technical skill set and a different psychological makeup than those that make you successful as a physician.[8]

Besides, even if you think you possess the right stuff to be a superior investor, it is not worth your time to find out. A typical doctor works 55 hours or more each week. He already has less free time than most people. Let's assume he has been in practice for four or five years, and has built up $250,000 in investments. Why not manage that portfolio himself, and save an advisor's fees?

Let's run the numbers. If he spends five hours a week on his investments, that adds up to 250 hours a year. Let's assume his research and active management work out, and he beats the markets, net of fees and costs, by 2% per year. (Not bloody likely, says the data, but let's proceed.)

He has made a profit from his investment skill of $5,000. So for each of his 250 hours of work, he's earned $20. Again, less than the waiter took home after the busy Friday night at T. G. I. Friday's. And this assumes he finds the persistent return advantage most professional investors fail to realize, instead of the large disadvantages experienced by most individual investors.

So keep your strategy simple and as nearly automatic as possible, especially starting out, when you don't have enough capital for superior investment performance to have meaningful impact

---

[8] Some psychological research suggests that *everyone* is systematically and consistently over-confident...except for those suffering from clinical depression, who are able to assess their own abilities very accurately. So you might want to be sure your investment advisor has a scrip for Zoloft.

anyway.

To get richer, faster, you simply need to save more.

Save your time and energy by adopting a simple investment strategy, choosing a limited number of core investments, and re-balancing your portfolio once a year.

Chapter 10: A Simple Plan

"Make everything as simple as possible, but not simpler."

Albert Einstein

Now you understand why trying to beat the market is a sub-optimal use of your scarce time and attention as a physician, especially in your early years in practice when you have only limited investment capital.

But what is the alternative? Should you just let money pile up in your bank accounts and leave it in a money-market fund in your retirement accounts?

Absolutely not. From the beginning of your investing career, you should follow a set of investing principles that will work for the rest of your life:

1) Diversify.

2) Invest the core of your portfolio is assets with the potential for real growth above inflation. In general, this means common stocks or mutual funds that invest primarily in common stocks. Inevitably, this means most of what you own will fluctuate in value.

3) Keep fees and costs low.

4) Think long-term and measure long-term. Ignore the short term. In fact, don't even open your statements if the market is going through a bad patch.

5) Utterly ignore volatility, headlines, CNBC, *The Wall Street*

Journal, Barron's, Mad Money with Jim Cramer; as well as any investment advice you receive from your colleagues, your patients, your golf buddy, or the investment banker in the paceline on your Sunday morning bike ride. (Especially ignore Jim Cramer.)

Let's turn these principles into a simple, practical investment strategy. For your retirement savings plan, we suggest the following simple asset allocation:[9]

- ➢ 40% S&P 500 Stock Index Fund.

- ➢ 30% Foreign Stock Index Fund *or* Foreign Large-Cap Value Fund.

- ➢ 20% Bond Index *or* Short-Term Bond Fund.

- ➢ 10% Money Market Fund *or* Guaranteed Investment Contract.

This strategy commits the core of your portfolio to common stocks, which have delivered superior returns over most long-term periods. It invests a large part of your growth assets outside the United States, reflecting the fact that we live in a competitive global economy, and the unfortunate reality that the U. S. faces significant economic policy challenges. Index funds are low-cost, and by definition will closely track the performance of the broad stock indexes. Short-term fixed-income and cash equivalents should reduce the portfolio's volatility by about one-third, making it easier to stick with your strategy when markets get scary.

Once a year, re-balance your accounts back to the baseline allocation above.

That's it. No 200-day moving averages, no Dow Theory buy and sell

---

[9] This is an illustrative target portfolio for a well-compensated investor, comfortable with risk, with an investment time horizon of a decade or more. It is not intended as a specific recommendation for any individual whose risk-tolerance and/or time horizon might be different.

signals, no market forecasts, no Power Lunches watching Maria Bartiromo, no covered-call writing, no newsletter subscriptions. No noise and nonsense.

With this simple strategy, we believe you will earn better returns than most individual investors. In your early years of practice, that is really all you need. *Instead of trying to beat the markets, focus on hitting your savings targets.*

Focusing on your savings rate, instead of on some complex investment strategy, also helps to highlight one of the most important, and most counter-intuitive, aspects of wealth accumulation. As a saver, you will be a *net buyer* of investment assets for at least the next two decades. Buyers always, *always* benefit from lower prices – for securities or commercial real estate, just as for skim milk or toilet paper. For savers, bear markets are good news; every bear market is an opportunity to buy quality assets on sale and get rich quicker.

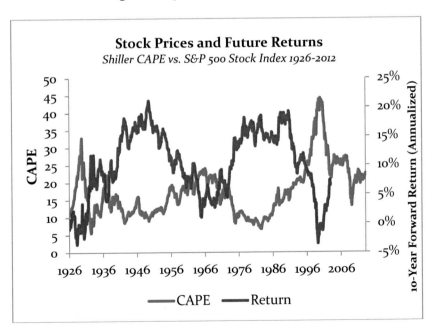

Stock Prices and Future Returns
Shiller CAPE vs. S&P 500 Stock Index 1926-2012

The chart above is a compelling visual of a simple truth about investing – *when stock prices are high, future returns will be low, and when stock prices are low, future returns will be high.*

The ideal fact-pattern for a retirement saver is a stock market that declines continuously until she retires, and then climbs continuously for the rest of her life. Obviously, neither of these scenarios (constant decline, constant increase) will happen. We just want you to be able to recognize the economic good news implicit in periodic bad news about markets and the economy.

We have been in the investment business since 1978. For most of that period, during the great bull market of 1982 to 2000, the investment winds were at our backs. For almost two decades, stock market returns averaging more than 17% a year piled up wealth as if by magic. Back then, high investment returns could make up for low savings rates.

Since 2000, the investment winds have been in our faces, not at our backs. That doesn't mean you can't build financial independence. But we can't expect investment miracles to make up for savings deficits, and we can't afford to squander any portion of today's modest investment returns by the typical individual investor's reactive, error-prone attempts at active investment management.

By making a limited set of positive, conscious and intentional decisions in your first year of medical practice, you can put yourself on the less-traveled road toward financial independence. We suggest that you focus on seven strategies during your first years of highly-compensated medical practice.

Chapter 11: The Seven Strategies

"Put the big rocks in first."

Chemistry professor to freshman students[10]

No choice, strategy or set of habits can guarantee a specific financial outcome, any more than you can guarantee admission to a specific medical school based on grade-point average. But there are best practices that can maximize your chances of getting the results you want.

We've observed the lives and habits of dozens of successful physicians over more than thirty years. We have identified seven strategies that can help point you toward financial success.

1) **Understand your actual cash flow.** (It will be less than you think.) As a resident and fellow with earnings under $50,000 per year, taxes took a relatively small bite. As a specialist with an income of $250,000 per year, your gross income may have increased by half an order of magnitude, but the actual cash flow you can spend will *not* be five times greater. Out of $250,000 of gross income, depending on the state in which you practice, you could easily be left with less than $150,000 per year after taxes, malpractice insurance, retirement savings and benefits costs.

2) **Get the basic protections in place first** – life insurance, disability insurance (to the extent it

---

[10] If you don't recognize this punchline to a very old story, send us an email and we will explain it.

remains available), property/casualty and umbrella liability insurance. Malpractice insurance, of course, if it is not already in place as part of your employment.

3) **Pay yourself first, and automatically.** For most physicians, this means contributing to a pre-tax retirement savings plan. It could be a 401k through an employer, or a self-employed retirement plan you set up yourself. Maximize pre-tax savings first, for both spouses. The percentage of income that you save will be the primary driver of your growth in net worth. *Only consider after-tax savings if you have already maxed-out your pre-tax retirement plans, and if you already have your insurance protections and your emergency fund in place.*

4) **Begin to build up an emergency cash reserve of three to six months of living expenses.** Even if you never have a financial emergency (as most of us do not), this reserve will have profound value in terms of how you see your finances. By putting dollars aside from each paycheck, instead of spending until your checking account is empty, you are training yourself to live below your means.

5) **Make sure you have a will, and update it to reflect your family situation and new income profile.** In working with your estate attorney, assume you've already accumulated several million dollars, and make the necessary provisions to safeguard and manage it. Hopefully in five or ten years you will have your million. In the midst of a busy career, it will be very easy to put off revising your will. So assume from the beginning that you are going to have meaningful assets, and plan for how to use them to protect those you love.

6) **Buy less house, in a good school district.** The

smartest buy is usually an understandable, well-built used house, not a trendy new McMansion. Get pre-qualified for a mortgage. Avoid money pits. To a much greater degree than you expect, the cost of upkeep and utilities will scale with the size and luxury of your home, and the extent and beauty of your grounds. Finance using a 30-year, fixed-rate mortgage.[11]

7) **Choose your friends wisely.** Remember the concept of *social comparison* – the more uniform and expensive the lifestyles of your friends, the higher the pressure to comply with the implicit status expectations of your peer group. Some of our most financially successful clients have the most eclectic groups of friends.

---

[11] In other financial guides for doctors, we've seen advice like, "Always finance with a 15-year or shorter mortgage." We disagree with this absolute. Sometimes a shorter-term mortgage is good, sometimes bad. If you can finance for 30 years at 3.75% tax-deductible, instead of for 15 years at 3.25%, and use the extra monthly cash flow to pay down a 6.8% medical school loan, there is absolutely no question you will be better off. When the med school loan is paid off, *then* you can aggressively pre-pay the 30-year mortgage. At the end of the day, this sequence will have *all* loans paid off sooner, and will minimize your total after-tax interest costs.

In a world where doctors struggle with rational pessimism about the future of the profession, we hope we have offered some reasons for rational long-term optimism about your personal finances. We wish you a happy, productive and prosperous future. *To your wealth.*

Chapter 12: The Advisor Advantage

"There are two ways to acquire wisdom. You can buy it, or you can rent it."

Benjamin Franklin

We live in the age of the Internet, which has both benefits and consequences. Among the benefits is easy access to a wealth of information on almost any topic imaginable. Among the negative consequences is an explosion of do-it-yourself activity, even in areas where training and experience have incalculable value.

What doctor has not had a conversation with a patient who suggests an alternative diagnosis or treatment, based on something he read on WebMD?

Just like the patients surfing WebMD on their iPads, you may well be inclined to act as your own financial advisor, using online resources to help you to make financial decisions and manage your portfolio.

We think this is usually a bad idea, for several reasons.

First, the urge to "do-it-yourself" violates one of the primary drivers of human intellectual and material progress – the principle of comparative advantage. The entire world gets richer when we each do what we are best at, and let others do what they do best.

Second, doing it yourself ignores one of the fundamental realities of life for physicians – their lack of time.

Third, and most important, doing it yourself requires you to make all of your own mistakes. As financial advisors who entered the business in 1978, and who have observed the financial decisions of hundreds of families over more than thirty years, we know exactly how costly it can be to learn-by-doing.

This kind of real-world experience is one of the principal benefits of having an advisor. You don't have to learn by trial and error, and you don't have to waste your scarce headspace getting up-to-speed on investing, insurance and the other technical aspects of personal finance in the 21st century. That time and attention is better spent keeping current with the advancing state of the medical art.

As a doctor starting practice, you need an advisor to perform six key functions:

1) Make sure you have put in place the necessary structures and protections for you and your family in the relatively unlikely event of death or disability.

2) Work with you to set realistic long-term goals, using best-practice financial modeling, and making realistic assumptions about future market returns.

3) Help you keep track of your progress, using metrics that distinguish between financial signal and market noise.

4) Manage your investments to successfully capture the economic returns available in the financial markets.

5) Be your trusted partner in making the financial decisions needed to build walk-away wealth, especially by helping you to avoid the costly unforced economic errors that so many doctors make early in their careers.

6) Provide accountability about hitting your net savings and capital accumulation targets, to make sure your actual financial behavior matches your sincere intentions. (Given the grim statistics on wealth accumulation for most physicians, this may

be the most important function of all.)

Notice what is *not* on this list. You don't need an advisor to beat the markets (few do), to protect you from portfolio declines (a hopeless task and in practice a sales pitch for high-cost insurance policies), or to help you discover the meaning of life.

You need someone who is intelligent and sensible, who will help you to put a solid structure in place, upon which you can build your financial security over decades. *You need to get on track early.*

We discussed earlier why insurance agents are often the first advisors to approach young doctors. The high commissions on whole-life insurance provide an attractive payday for an insurance agent. What often results is a physician with good disability insurance coverage, a $10,000 per year premium for a whole life insurance policy she eventually realizes she does not need, and a lasting skepticism about financial advisors.

What *doesn't* happen is a systematic approach to the payment of debts, setup of savings plans, purchase of a house, and establishment of a network of advisors.

You absolutely need the proper sorts of insurance, especially if you are married, even more so if you have children. But your principal advisor should not earn much of his compensation from commissions on insurance sales – or sales of any other financial product or service, for that matter. The potential for conflict of interest is simply too great.

Until recently, there was no fee-based compensation model designed to deliver competent and objective advice to the group of physicians who need it the most – young doctors starting practice. We believe that is changing, and we hope to help that process along. This book is part of our solution.

Afterword

"The journey of a thousand miles begins with a single step."

Lao Tzu

In this little book, we have tried to clarify some of the key moving parts of the transition from poorly-paid residency or fellowship to well-paid practice in a medical sub-specialty.

We hope we have helped you to understand how the specific choices you make in your first year in practice -- as you are moving, buying a house, furniture and cars, signing up for your employer savings plan, and assembling your team of advisors -- can put you on track toward walk-away financial independence by normal retirement age.

- ➤ If you have any suggestions about how this guide could be improved, please email us at feedback@tgsfin.com.

- ➤ If you would like information about *Triage*, our fee-based advisory program for young physicians, email us at questions@tgsfin.com, or go to the *Triage* web-site at www.tgstriage.com.

- ➤ If you would like to schedule an initial consultation with one of our financial advisors, please call us at (800) 525-4075.

Since the founding of TGS Financial Advisors in 1990, helping physicians achieve better financial outcomes has been a key focus of our independent advisory practice. If you wish to explore how we can help you manage your finances today, to help you create better choices twenty years from now, we would welcome the opportunity to meet with you,

About the Authors

David A. Burd, CFP®
A graduate of Swarthmore College, David has worked in the investment field since 1978. He holds the CERTIFIED FINANCIAL PLANNER™ certification. He co-founded TGS Financial Advisors with Jim Hemphill in 1990.

David's practice concentrates on the financial needs of physicians and medical specialists. David was named as one of *The Best Financial Advisers for Doctors* by *Medical Economics* magazine in 2006, 2010, 2011, 2012, and 2013.

David is married to Charlene, who has a Master's in Education and is a counselor in the Delran Middle School in New Jersey. They have two children, Zachary and Samantha. They live in Voorhees, New Jersey.

James S. Hemphill, CFP®, CIMA
Jim graduated from Swarthmore College. He has been managing investment portfolios since 1978. He co-founded TGS Financial Advisors with David Burd in 1990.

Jim holds the CERTIFIED FINANCIAL PLANNER™, and Certified Investment Management Analyst certifications.

Jim's practice focuses on successfully managing the retirement transition, especially for successful entrepreneurs selling a business. He serves as the firm's Chief Investment Strategist. For his up to date thoughts on the markets and investment strategy, visit his blog, *The Glass Half Full*.

Jim is married to Amy, who received her Master of Public Health from Johns Hopkins University in 1998. They have two sons, Jack and Alex, and a daughter, Katharine. They live in West Chester, Pennsylvania.

18145277R00041

Made in the USA
San Bernardino, CA
02 January 2015